Can you find the hotel?

This is the village of Kippen.

It is in Main Street.

The Cross Keys Hotel is in Main Street.
Main Street is in Kippen.

This is a map of Kippen.
The map tells you about Kippen.
It shows buildings, roads and gardens.

Cross Keys Hotel
Main Street
Kippen

This is the Cross Keys Hotel in Kippen.

Kippen is in the British Isles.

The British Isles

This is a photo of the British Isles.
It shows land and water.

This is a map of the British Isles.
It shows land and water.

North West Highlands

Grampian Mountains

River Tay

North Sea

Lake District

Pennines

Mourne Mountains

River Trent

River Shannon

Irish Sea

Cambrian Mountains

River Severn

River Thames

Macgillycuddy's Reeks

There are rivers in the British Isles.
There are hills and mountains.
The map shows some of them.

Edinburgh
Glasgow
Newcastle upon Tyne
Belfast
Leeds
Dublin
Liverpool
Manchester
Birmingham
Norwich
Cardiff
London
Bristol

There are cities in the British Isles.
The map shows some of them.

flag of the
Republic of Ireland

flag of the
United Kingdom

United

Kingdom

Republic
of
Ireland

Dublin

London

The British Isles are made up of the United Kingdom and
the Republic of Ireland.
Each country has a capital city. Each country has a flag.

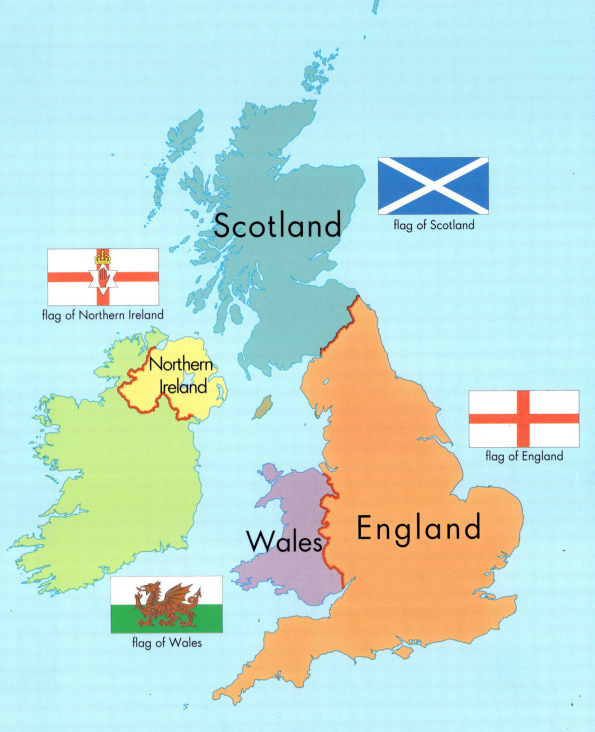

Scotland

flag of Scotland

flag of Northern Ireland

Northern Ireland

flag of England

Wales

England

flag of Wales

There are four countries in the United Kingdom.
Each country has a flag.

The British Isles are part of Europe.
This is a part of Europe.

Rivers, hills and mountains

North
Sea

River
Rhine

Carpathian
Mountains

The Alps

River
Danube

Pyrenees

Mediterranean Sea

This is a map of Europe.
There are rivers and mountains in Europe.

Stockholm

Dublin

London

Berlin

Warsaw

Paris

Vienna

Madrid

Rome

Athe...

There are cities in Europe.
The map shows some of the cities.

Sweden

Republic
of
Ireland

U.K.

Germany

Poland

France

Austria

Spain

Italy

Greece

There are countries in Europe.
Some of the countries are named.

Europe is part of the Earth.

These are photos of the Earth from space.

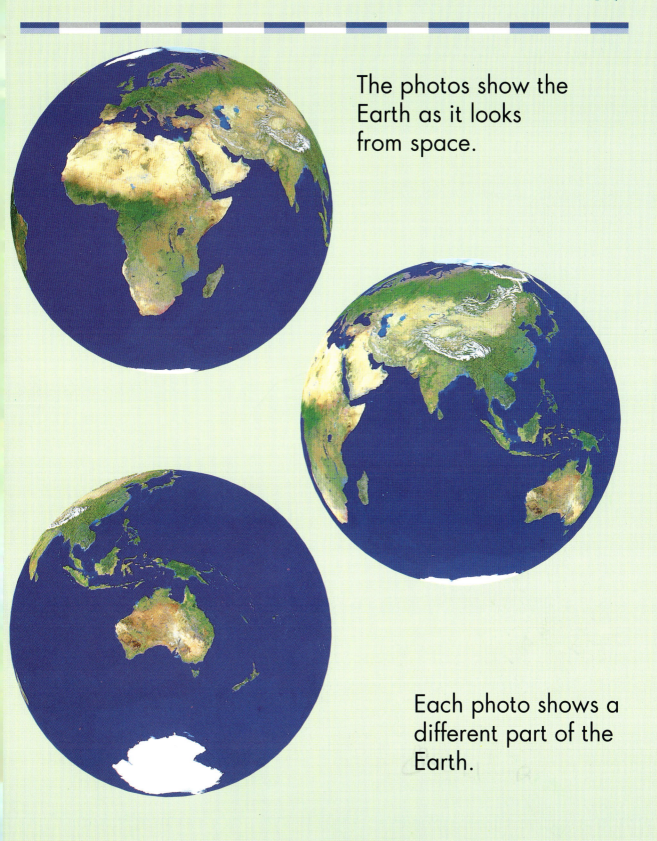

The photos show the Earth as it looks from space.

Each photo shows a different part of the Earth.

Arctic

North
America

Atlantic
Ocean

Pacific
Ocean

South
America

Atlantic
Ocean

The Earth is also called the World.
This is a map of the World.
It shows all of the World.

Ocean

Europe

Asia

Africa

Pacific
Ocean

Indian
Ocean

Oceania

Southern Ocean

Antarctica

This map shows land and water.
The huge areas of land are called continents.
The huge areas of water are called oceans.

Rocky
Mountains

River
Mississippi

Saha...

River
Amazon

Andes

This map of the World shows some rivers and mountains.
It names some deserts.

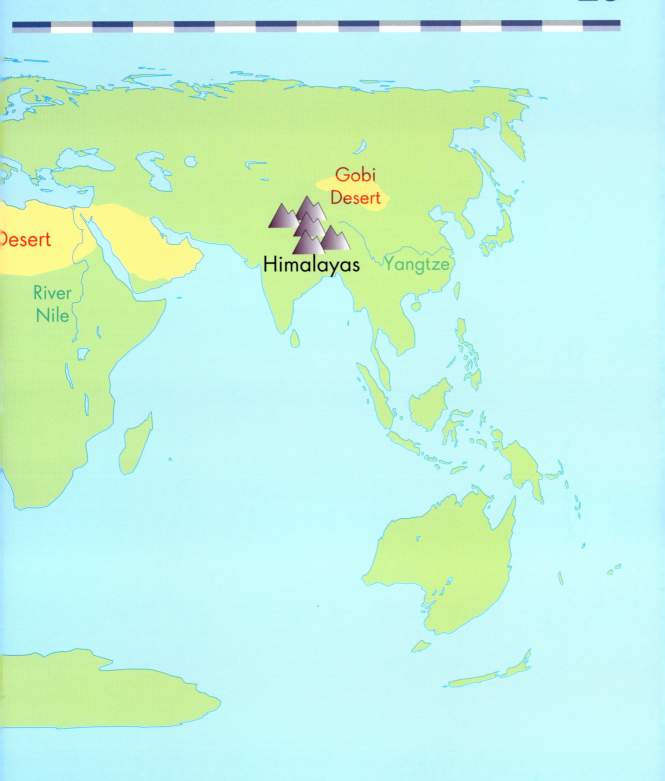

Gobi
Desert

Desert

Himalayas

Yangtze

River
Nile

London
Paris

New York

U.S.A.

Nigeria

Brazil

Buenos Aires

There are many cities in the World.
Some of the cities are named on the map.